AF207902

When God Shows Up

When God Shows Up

Discovering God in Stories of Hope

A STORYTELLERS LIVE BIBLE STUDY SERIES

PUBLISHED BY

StoryTellers Live: WHEN GOD SHOWS UP:
DISCOVERING GOD IN STORIES OF HOPE
Copyright © 2021 by StoryTellers Live
Published by Iron Hill Press in the United States of America.

ISBN: 979-8-9857498-8-5

Library of Congress Cataloging-in-Publication Data is on file at the Library of Congress, Washington, DC.

Unless otherwise noted, all Scripture the Holy Bible, New International Version® NIV® Copyright © 1973, 1978, 1984, 2011 by Biblica, Inc.® Used by permission. All rights reserved worldwide.

English Standard Version® (ESV®) © 2001 by Crossway, a publishing ministry of Good News Publishers. All rights reserved.

Author: Katie Dunn
Design: Dawn Curtis, Ruth Book Designing, Upper Air Creative
Cover Artwork: Rushton Waltchack

Contents

StoryTellers Live

Everyday women sharing stories of hope found in Jesus

- **Live Gatherings**

  StoryTellers Live has communities across the country where women share personal stories of God's love and encourage one another in their faith journey.

- **Podcast**

  The stories from the live gatherings are aired on the StoryTellers Live podcast to empower women around the world to see God more clearly in the details of their lives and discover His goodness, trustworthiness, and faithfulness.

- **Biblical Resources**

  StoryTellers Live offers Bible studies and other resources to equip women with God's Word and help them discover the intimacy of a relationship with God.

FOR MORE INFORMATION ON OUR EVENTS, PODCASTS, AND LINKS TO OUR SOCIAL MEDIA VISIT:

STORYTELLERSLIVE.ORG

StoryTellers Live, Inc. is a 501(c)(3) organization. 100% of donations go towards expenses for our operation.

Welcome

A Message from the StoryTellers Live podcast hosts

From the *StoryTellers Live Podcast Team*, welcome and thank you for choosing to spend the next eight weeks with us as you begin **When God Shows Up: Discovering God in Stories of HOPE.** We pray as you go through this study and you hear how God showed up in the lives of these eight women, you will experience God in a new and profound way. Most importantly, we pray that as you see Him in the storylines of others, you will in turn see Him in the storylines of your life as well.

Over and over again in the gospels, Jesus revealed the mysteries of God's Kingdom through the power of stories. He called them parables, and He didn't say anything to His followers without using them (Mark 4:34). Jesus told these stories to teach those who sought after Him and help them understand who He was and how they played a role in building His Kingdom. Jesus used earthly stories to speak Heavenly truths.

Today, God still speaks to us through the power of story, and He often uses ordinary people, like you and me, to tell others about who He is. As you listen to the stories previously recorded at a *StoryTellers Live* gathering, you will see how God moves when a person speaks truthfully, honestly, and vulnerably from the heart. It is compelling, extraordinarily moving, and has the ability to change lives. After all, as you will soon experience, **WHEN GOD SHOWS UP**, everything changes because He changes everything! Thank you again for entrusting us with your time and know we are praying for you as you begin this journey.

Lindy, Robyn & Katie

The Storytellers Live Podcast Team

"Always be prepared to give an answer to everyone who asks you to give the reason for the HOPE that you have. But do this with gentleness and respect."

1 Peter 3: 15

Before you Begin

You are going to hear real and personal stories from eight different women. You will find some of the stories you listen to profound and challenging. Other stories you will find more common and relatable. You will laugh with some. You will cry with others. In the end, you will see God's transforming love and how our Creator is in the business of exchanging ordinary for EXTRAORDINARY and broken for REDEEMED.

In each session of this guide, you will find five sections - each section is listed below with details on how you can get the most out of your small group time as well as your individual study.

Before your small group time, go through the first three sections of each session:

THINK ABOUT IT

This section includes two opening questions. These questions will get you thinking about where the storyteller is heading in her podcast and how God can use her story to speak truth directly to you. These questions can be used for your own personal reflection to prepare your heart for where the storyteller is headed in her story, or, if your group feels led to discuss these, they can also be revisited in your small group time.

LISTEN TO THE PODCAST

Find each podcast on our website at **www.storytellerslive.org/ storiesofhope**. Each podcast will take about 40-50 minutes to listen to. You can listen at your leisure … in your car, as you fold your laundry, as you take a walk, the opportunities are endless. In this section of your study guide, you will find quotes taken directly from the storyteller. You can use these quotes to follow along or to review during your small group time (some of these quotes may even become sticky note reminders for your bathroom mirror).

ALL podcasts can be found at
www.storytellerslive.org/storiesofhope

STUDY THROUGH SCRIPTURE

Reflect upon what God has taught you. These questions provide an opportunity to dig deeper into Scripture and reflect upon what God has taught you through the storyteller. It is our prayer that these questions will allow you to encounter God on a personal level as He reveals Himself to you through His Word.

The final two sections are for your small group time:

OPENING UP AND BEING REAL - A TIME TO SHARE

These questions create an opportunity for you to discuss with your small group all God has revealed to you as you listened to the podcast and as you delved into Scripture over the themes of the story you heard.

At **StoryTellers Live**, we believe we were designed to experience life in community with others. So, we encourage you to share with your small group as you feel led, but you can also use these questions to reflect upon individually with the Lord.

We would suggest allowing 45 minutes for discussion. This creates time for everyone to participate. You can pick and choose which questions you discuss, or use them all as time permits.

If you are a small group leader, be sure you look over these questions and have some responses prepared in order to get the discussion flowing. Also, as a leader it is imperative you make your small group time a "safe" place to share. Emphasize the importance of trust within the group, and make sure participants understand that what is said in the group stays in the group.

Each week, after you finish your discussion with your small group, you, or someone in your group, can close your time together by praying over the group. Feel free to use the prompts in this section as you feel led. This is also a great time to ask for specific prayer requests within your group if anyone feels comfortable sharing.

Again, thank you for choosing to entrust us with your time over the next eight weeks. God's Word tells us that it never returns void (Isaiah 55:11), and we are confident you will experience His intimacy and faithfulness as you go through the study. So, get ready to be encouraged in your faith, strengthened in your trust, and overwhelmed by the majesty of a Father who desires for you to place your HOPE in Him alone!

Katie Dunn

Author of the "When God Shows Up" series

—SESSION ONE—

JESSICA

"Longing to Be Known: An Army Widow's Story"

"You have searched me, Lord, and You know me."

Psalm 139:1

When God shows up, you discover He sees you and knows you by name.

Think About It

Questions to consider before and after you listen to the podcast.

In what ways do we tend to put people in the place of Savior?

____

____

____

How can placing our hope in the things of this world be like building a house on shifting sand?

____

____

____

Listen to the Podcast

"Jessica: Longing to Be Known - An Army Widow's Story"
Find the podcast at www.storytellerslive.org/storiesofhope

Storyteller Podcast Highlights

- *"Rest on embalmed and sainted dead! Dear is the blood you gave; No impious footstep here shall tread in the herbage of your grave."*
- *I became an army wife and I was really good at it.*
- *He kissed me and I said please come home and he never did.*
- *My identity was being crushed completely. Everything I had built my life up in was not eternal.*
- *Psalm 139 - God met me to remind me He was watching all of this and He was allowing it so I would find who I was in Him.*
- *God was using grief to save me from sin.*
- *Today, I no longer live. Christ lives in me.*

Study the Story in Scripture

Allow God's Word to transform your heart, mind, and soul as you spend time alone with Him.

Jessica longed to be "known." Her longing was satisfied when she became known as an army wife, but this was stripped away when her husband was killed in action. Being known by God is the only solid place we can find security and comfort in this world. It is a truth you must revisit every day. Choose any of the following verses and write out how they speak truth to you.

Luke 12:6-7

1 Corinthians 8:3; 13:12

John 10:27-30

Nahum 1:7

How does it make you feel knowing the God of the universe knows every hair on your head (**Matthew 10:30**) and that no trial you endure escapes His eyes?

____

____

____

It's easy to place people in your life in the place of "Savior." Read **Psalm 33:13-22**. How do these verses speak to you in where you are placing your hope?

____

____

____

God desires to be the solid foundation on which we build our lives. Read the following verses and write out what this foundation provides for you in times of need.

Isaiah 28:16

____

____

Psalm 61:2

____

____

Psalm 62:6

____

____

Luke 6:46-49

____

____

Ephesians 2:19-22

____

____

1 Corinthians 3:10-11

____

____

1 Peter 2:4-8

____

____

Jessica got excited when she first read **2 Timothy 3:16**, "All Scripture is God-breathed and is useful for teaching, rebuking, correcting and training in righteousness." In light of this verse, take some time to read **Psalm 139**. Write out what God is teaching you through these verses, how they may rebuke any lies from Satan, how they may correct any incorrect thinking, and how they can train you up in righteousness.

Jessica ends her story by saying she no longer lives, but Christ lives in her. Read **Galatians 2:20**. What does it mean to you to be "crucified with Christ" and to "live by faith in the Son of God"?

How can you take steps in living out **Galatians 2:20** on a daily basis?

____

____

____

How does recognizing you are known by God increase your HOPE in Him as Savior?

____

____

____

For your small group time:

Opening Up and Being Real

Build community within your small group as you discuss the themes of the podcast.

- What resonated with you about Jessica's story? Why?

- Without any context of Christ in her life, as a young adult, Jessica filled her life with whatever pleased her. Has there ever been a time in your life where you found yourself "apathetic about everything"?

- Jessica said once she moved to Fort Bragg, she became an army wife and "was really good at it." How can we keep ourselves in check when it comes to finding our identity in our jobs or in our positions in our families?

- When the Secretary of the Army showed up to formally tell Jessica her husband had been killed in action, all Jessica heard was "you don't exist anymore." Have you ever experienced something so devastating you thought your life was over? How did you recover from it?

- Jessica said over the next several days that passed, she was being held up by a strength she couldn't describe - one that prevented her from drowning herself in behaviors that would keep her from feeling anything. How has God showed up in ways you couldn't describe in moments of deep sorrow?

- After Tel passed away, Jessica said "everything I built my life upon was not eternal." What does Matthew 7:24-27 say we should build our lives on? How does having Jesus as our foundation keep us secure in times of struggle?

- After the funeral, God met Jessica in her grief and spoke to her through His Word. Jessica said, "He was allowing it (her grief) so I could find who I was in Him." She said her grief saved her from her sin. Has grief ever exposed your sin or pointed out your need for a Savior?

- Jessica said God "sees us and knows us and loves us anyway." How does this statement speak truth to you today?

Closing Your Small Group Time with Prayer

Spend time in worship as you reflect on what God has taught you through the storyteller and His Word.

Take time as a group to pray in any of the following directions:

Praise God for the story He brought you through Jessica. Praise Him for being the only solid foundation upon which you can build your life. Praise God for His Word and the foundation Scripture provides for your daily life. Praise Him for His Holy Spirit and how that Spirit guides you to this foundation.

Ask God for forgiveness for the times in which you placed others above Him or when you built your life on the things of this world.

Thank God for meeting you right where you are in your walk with Him. Thank Him for the moments in which He has used your grief to save you from your sin and to draw you closer to Him. Thank Him for the eternal home He is preparing for you. Thank Him for fully knowing you and loving you.

Pray for God to give you a desire to know Him more and that He would draw you closer to Him. Ask God to be your solid foundation in every aspect of life. Ask Him to help you live your life out of His security and comfort alone.

SESSION TWO

KATIE

"Releasing Her Children's Choices"

When God shows up, you discover how to trust Him with your life and those you love.

Think About It

Questions to consider before and after you listen to the podcast.

What do you think is the difference between head knowledge of God and heart knowledge of Him?

____

____

____

In what ways do you feel your children's successes or failures are a reflection of you?

____

____

____

Listen to the Podcast

"Katie: Releasing Her Children's Choices"
Find the podcast at www.storytellerslive.org/storiesofhope

Storyteller Podcast Highlights

- Being a mom became my purpose in life; it was where I found my identity.
- I was responsible for everything they did - good and bad.
- God's the one who writes their testimony, not me.
- This stupid decision my child made ... God used it to really shape me and teach me so many truths about who He is.
- I cannot make my children's choices. They aren't my robots, just like I'm not God's robot.
- I don't worry about what people think of me, and I certainly don't worry about what they think of my child.
- God will give you enough faith for your present reality, not your imagination.

Study the Story in Scripture

Allow God's Word to transform your heart, mind, and soul as you spend time alone with Him.

One of the most prominent themes in Scripture is "trust in God," especially in moments when the future seems so uncertain. The definition of trust is "a firm belief in the reliability, truth, ability, or strength of someone." One way to build this "firm belief" in God is to habitually spend time in His Word. How do the following verses speak truth to you regarding trusting your Heavenly Father?

Joshua 1:9

____

____

Isaiah 26:3

____

____

Jeremiah 17:7-8

____

____

Psalm 37:4-6

____

____

Psalm 56:3

____

____

Psalm 112:7

____

____

Proverbs 29:25

____

____

Hebrews 13:8

____

____

Katie held on to Psalm 9:10 as she learned to trust God. What does this verse say to you?

____

____

____

Relinquishing control is really rooted in fear; usually fear of the unknown. What is God laying on your heart right now that you need to give control to Him?

____

____

____

The story of Balaam and the donkey is found in **Numbers 22:21-35**. Have there been moments in your life (or in your children's lives) where you were trying to "make the donkey go" and it wouldn't? Did you trust God was in control or did you continue "beating" the donkey to control the situation?

Balaam thought he was doing what God wanted him to do, but he went out on his journey without going to God first in prayer asking for guidance. How have you followed God in a situation, only to take the reins and go out on your own without conversing with Him? What was the result?

____

____

____

Katie said she found her biggest weapon in raising her children was prayer. The Apostle Paul tells us in Ephesians 6:18 that "praying always" is essentially a wartime activity. End today, crying out to God as if you were in a war. Write out your worries, concerns, control issues, and lay your "picture" at His feet. Rest in knowing He hears your prayer, He is faithful to respond, and He will fight on your behalf!

How does your HOPE in the Lord allow you to trust your life and those you love completely to God?

____

____

____

For your small group time:

Opening Up and Being Real ——————

Build community within your small group as you discuss the themes of the podcast.

- What resonated with you about Katie's story? Why?

- Katie said she found her identity in being a mom. How can finding our identity in the things of this world set us up for disappointment?

- One of the reasons we can't find fulfillment in ourselves (or in those around us) is because we were created to reflect the glory of God. When we seek to find an identity in something outside of Christ, we are really seeking to bring glory to ourselves - and, we will never find lasting fulfillment apart from Him. Where are you tempted to find your identity?

• How does the question, "Do you believe 'in' God or do you believe God" speak to you?

• Katie mentioned the many control issues she had when her children were in elementary and middle school. Do you struggle with control issues- whether it is in your life, or your spouse, or your children, or your friends? If so, how has this control issue affected you? How has it affected the relationships around you?

• Like Katie, do you have a "picture" you are wanting for yourself or your family? When things don't work out according to your picture, how do you react?

• Katie said she has learned God is the one who writes her children's testimonies, not her. How does knowing God is in the business of writing testimonies free you as a follower of Christ?

• Have you ever let your imagination run wild with "what ifs" concerning your life? How does the statement, "God will give you enough faith in your present reality, not your imagination" combat these movies we tend to play in our heads?

Closing Your Small Group Time with Prayer

Spend time in worship as you reflect on what God has taught you through the storyteller and His Word.

Take time as a group to pray in any of the following directions:

Praise God for the story He brought you through Katie. Praise Him for the family He has blessed you with and the uniqueness of each family member. Praise Him for how He disciplines you and continues to teach you about who He is.

Ask God for forgiveness when you have tried to take the driver's seat of your life and the ones you love. Ask Him for forgiveness when you have failed to trust Him in the details of your life. Ask Him for forgiveness when you have lived out of disbelief.

Thank God that He is in the business of writing testimonies and bringing salvation to the world and that the burden is not placed on you. Thank Him for being a God who is trustworthy and who never forsakes those who seek Him. Thank Him for giving you enough faith for your present reality.

Pray God would help you relinquish control of your life and the ones you love to Him. Ask Him to help you let go of the "picture" you have in your mind of how your life and the lives of the ones you love should look. Pray He would draw closer to you as you draw closer to Him through this study.

SESSION THREE

AMY W

"Faith Above Works"

> *"He will cover you with His feathers, and under His wings you will find refuge; His faithfulness will be your shield and rampart."*
>
> Psalm 9:10

When God shows up, you discover His free gift of grace.

Think About It

Questions to consider before and after you listen to the podcast.

Have you ever struggled with the thought that you aren't "good enough" for God?

____

____

____

Do you ever let your past define who you are today?

____

____

____

Listen to the Podcast

"Amy W: Faith Above Works"
Find the podcast at www.storytellerslive.org/storiesofhope

StoryTeller Podcast Highlights

- Assigned the role to myself of a "good works" kid, but sometimes the right heart can go in the wrong direction.
- God made me understand what salvation really was.
- I was a "good works" kid, constantly trying to win the favor of people and the favor of God. When those "good works" are stripped away, it's just you and God.
- God likes to get in our messes and make miracles out of them.

Study the Story in Scripture

Allow God's Word to transform your heart, mind, and soul as you spend time alone with Him.

Amy found her identity in being a "good works" kid, but the problem with that is we were created to find our identity in Christ, and in Him alone. As a child of God, born again through the blood of Christ, it is imperative you know how God sees you and how His view of you never changes. Read the following verses and write down what God's Word says about your identity.

John 1:12

Ephesians 1:3-14

1 Peter 4:16

Romans 6:8-11

You are a child of God, a citizen of Heaven, forgiven, and alive to God in Jesus Christ. These truths are all a reflection of God's grace. How does this grace free you from acting as if you are responsible for your acceptance into God's presence and His Kingdom?

____

____

____

Read **Ephesians 2:4-9**. What do these verses tell you about your salvation? How are you saved? How do these verses free you from a "good works" mentality?

____

____

____

Read **2 Timothy 1:9**. What did we do for God to save us? According to this verse, how are we saved?

____

____

____

Salvation is nothing short of a divine exchange - our filthy rags of self-effort for the perfection of Jesus Christ. As Amy said, "God doesn't measure our deservedness the way we do." When you spend time reflecting on this gift from God, what emotions arise in you?

____

____

____

How does this gift of saving grace free you to love God more intimately and serve Him more intently?

____

____

____

Have you ever disqualified yourself for future Kingdom work because of your past mistakes?

____

____

____

What truth does **Psalm 103:8-12** reveal to you?

____

____

____

Amy spoke about how God can make miracles out of our messes. Write out **Romans 8:28**.

____

____

____

How has God worked your past mistakes for good?

____

____

____

Continue reading in **Romans 8** to verses **31-39**. How do these verses speak to you regarding your past, your future, and the love of your Heavenly Father?

Our HOPE in God allows us to accept His free gift of grace. Do you struggle with accepting this gift? If you answered yes, explain why? If you answered no, take a moment to thank God for this gift.

____

____

Opening Up and Being Real

Build community within your small group as you discuss the themes of the podcast.

- What resonated with you about Amy's story? Why?

- Amy shared a comment a boy said to her when she was in 10th grade, and it still made her emotional. Why do you think negative comments given to us about ourselves stick around so much longer than the positive ones?

- When someone suggested Amy consider adoption, her initial thought was "I couldn't possibly adopt" because she thought she wasn't "good enough." Satan loves to keep us stagnant in our walk with Christ with this lie. Have you ever struggled with a "couldn't possibly" because you didn't think you were "good enough"?

- God taught Amy about His salvation through the adoption of Landry. How has God come into your mess and saved you from yourself? How has He provided for you what you couldn't provide for yourself?

- Because Amy thought her story wasn't "perfect," she was afraid of sharing it with others. What, if anything, keeps you from telling your story to others?

- Amy clung to **Psalm 91:4** and recognized God had protected her in many of her choices. Looking back at your life, have you seen God's hand of protection over you?

- Amy spoke about how God had ordained everything in her book of life and how He was able to "restore all the years the locust ate." Do you believe this statement? How has God taken your past pain, brokenness, and loneliness and brought good from it?

Closing Your Small Group Time with Prayer

Spend time in worship as you reflect on what God has taught you through the storyteller and His Word.

Take time as a group to pray in any of the following directions:

Praise God for the story He brought you through Amy. Praise Him for His incredible gift of grace, forgiveness, and faith. Praise Him for being an intimate Father who is our refuge and protection.

Ask God for forgiveness in moments where you have placed your works above your faith. Ask Him for forgiveness when you have lived out of the lies of this world. Ask God for forgiveness when you have disqualified yourself from Kingdom work because of the choices you've made.

Thank God for not measuring "deservedness" the way the world does. Thank Him for being a God who can restore "lost" years. Thank Him for making miracles out of messes.

Pray God would allow you to see yourself and your future the way He does. Pray He would help you understand salvation more clearly and the divine gift it represents. Pray God would allow you to begin to see how He can make miracles out of the messes in your life.

SESSION FOUR

LINDY

"Surrendering Her Agenda: A Breast Cancer Story"

"God is within her, she will not fall; God will help her at break of day."

Psalm 46:5

**When God shows up, you discover
the freedom found in surrendering.**

Think About It

Questions to consider before and after you listen to the podcast.

Has something unexpected ever happened in your life where you thought,
"God, I just don't have time for this!"?

____

____

____

Do you allow God to control your schedule or do you control it?

____

____

____

Listen to the Podcast

"Lindy: Surrendering Her Agenda - A Breast Cancer Story"
Find the podcast at www.storytellerslive.org/storiesofhope

StoryTeller Podcast Highlights

- When I had my first mammogram at 42, I was called back in for a
  re-check. I thought, "I don't have time for this."
- Before I got the results, I heard God say, "It's positive, but I've got this."
- It was a matter of surrender. Who's plan was it? Was it my plan or God's
  plan?
- I still tried to control everything.
- After surgery, I had to be still.
- What do you have time for?
- Who's plan is it?
- Where do you get your worth?

Study the Story in Scripture

Allow God's Word to transform your heart, mind, and soul as you spend time alone with Him.

A common theme throughout Scripture is the encouragement to surrender to God. To surrender means to yield to the power of another; to relinquish control over what you consider yours - meaning your property, your time, your "rights." When you surrender to God, you acknowledge all these things actually belong to Him. Read the following verses and write what God tells you about surrendering your life to Him.

Jeremiah 10:23-24

____

____

Mark 14:35-36

____

____

John 3:30; 15:5

____

____

Romans 6:6; 6:13; 12:1

____

____

Luke 1:38; 9:23-24

____

____

James 4:10

____

____

1 Peter 5:6-10

____

____

In light of this definition and the previous verses, what is God calling you to surrender?

____

____

What is holding you back from surrendering every aspect of your life to God?

____

____

Recognizing God is in control of everything can also give you freedom from worrying about your present circumstances. What fears/anxieties do you need to surrender to God today?

____

____

Lindy posed three questions at the end of her story. Spend this week reflecting on the following questions and listen to what God is saying to you. Use the space below to journal as needed.

____

____

What do you have time for? "I can tell a lot about you if I look at your calendar and your checkbook." What are your passions and pursuits, and where do your strengths lie?

____

____

What is your personal mission?

____

____

Where do you want to spend your time?

____

____

Whose plan is it?

____

____

Do you trust the Lord in the details of your life?

____

____

What do you do when the plan doesn't match what you think the reality should be?

____

____

Where do you get your worth?

____

____

God created you for His glory. Do you live this way?

____

____

What are you telling your children about their self-worth? "If you're identity isn't in Christ, you're going to sink."

____

____

How can HOPE in God allow you to surrender your time, your agenda, and your self-worth to Him?

____

____

For your small group time:

Opening Up and Being Real

Build community within your small group as you discuss the themes of the podcast.

- What resonated with you about Lindy's story? Why?

- "I don't have time for this" is a theme for many people today. Has God ever called you to do something for Him where you said, "Later God, I promise, when I have time, I will get around to that"? If your answer is yes, what opportunities do you think you have missed as a result of your delay?

- For the first time in her life, Lindy clearly heard God speak to her when He said her results would be positive, but He's got this. Has there ever been a time in your life where you have heard God speak to you? If so, and if you feel comfortable, share with the group.

- Lindy said her breast cancer diagnosis was never a matter of life and death, but it was a matter of surrender. How has God called you to moments of surrender in your life?

- Even after Lindy knew she needed to surrender to God, she still tried to control her outcome. Why do you think we tend to think our plan is better than God's?

- God placed specific people in Lindy's life to calm her fears of the TRAM flap surgery. Have you ever experienced God's reassurance in moments where you were fearful? If so, how did that reassurance increase your trust in Him?

- Read Psalm 46:1-5. How do these verses reassure you of God's protection, provision, and faithfulness?

Closing Your Small Group Time with Prayer

Spend time in worship as you reflect on what God has taught you through the storyteller and His Word.

Take time as a group to pray in any of the following directions:

Praise God for the story He brought you through Lindy. Praise Him for being Jehovah-Rapha - the God Who heals. Praise Him for being a God who is trustworthy to surrender your life to, and One who is in control in the midst of surprise chaos.

Ask God for forgiveness for not surrendering every aspect of your life to Him. Ask Him for forgiveness when you've unknowingly told Him "I don't have time for this." Ask Him for forgiveness when you have thought your plan was better than His.

Thank God for speaking directly into your life through His Word. Thank Him for His presence in your life and for being your "helper at the break of day." Thank Him for His sovereignty and His provision.

Pray God would help you to surrender your entire life to Him - your time, your plan, and your self-worth. Ask Him to prepare you now for moments when unexpected change occurs. If you are in a season where fear is real, ask God to reassure you and increase your trust in His plan for your life.

SESSION FIVE

COURTNEY

"Removing the Masks and Crying Out to God"

> *"Give thanks to the Lord, for He is good; His love endures forever.*
> *Let the redeemed of the Lord tell their story."*
> Psalm 107:1-2a

When God shows up, you discover the joy of being authentic, vulnerable, and real.

Think About It

Questions to consider before and after you listen to the podcast.

Have you ever found yourself hiding behind a mask, telling everyone, "I'm fine," when you are really crumbling on the inside?

____

____

____

Why do you think people tend to withhold what's really going on in their lives?

____

____

____

Listen to the Podcast

"Courtney: Removing the Masks and Crying Out to God"
Find the podcast at www.storytellerslive.org/storiesofhope

StoryTeller Podcast Highlights

- I have a plethora of stories, which one to tell? One thing you have to do is make a timeline and see where God showed up
- I knew about God, but I didn't understand the difference between knowing about God and knowing God.
- I listened to the women tell their stories, and I thought I don't have a story like that. That Redeemer they are talking about, I don't know Him like that, and I want to know who He is.
- I felt very strongly that if "life-serving" God looked like this, I didn't want any part of it.
- The layer of masks I wore were impressive because I could hide any pain and struggle I was going through until one day I couldn't hide anymore.
- I found myself crying out to God saying, "if this is my story, if this is my son's

story, if this is Your story God, then I surrender." I realized in that moment that God's plan is perfect.

- My Friend, my Comforter is on the throne and whenever I feel weak, He reminds me, "Courtney, do you trust me" and my answer now and forever will be "yes, I do."

Study the Story in Scripture

Allow God's Word to transform your heart, mind, and soul as you spend time alone with Him.

Courtney spoke of exchanging the following four "worldly" masks (fear, shame, doubt, control) with four "God-given" masks (peace, surrender, trust, vulnerability). One of the best ways to reach for our "God-given" masks is to bathe ourselves in Scripture. Look up the following verses related to the mask exchange and record what God's Word says to you about each.

Replacing fear with peace

Deuteronomy 31:6; Romans 8:15-18; John 14:27; Phil. 4:6-8; 2 Thessalonians 3:16

____

____

Replacing shame with surrender

Psalm 32; Jeremiah 10:23; Matthew 16:24-25

____

____

Replacing doubt with trust

Proverbs 3:5-6; Psalm 143:8; John 14:1; John 20:26-29

____

____

Replacing control with vulnerability

Luke 12:22-26; James 4:10; Mark 8:35; 2 Corinthians 4:7

____

____

As Courtney surrendered her story and her son's story to God, she commented, "I have never felt so much strength and weakness in my life." The Apostle Paul spoke of this strength/weakness correlation in his second letter to the church in Corinth. Paul had been pleading to the Lord for Him to remove "the thorn in his flesh." Three times Paul pleaded, but the thorn was not removed. Read **2 Corinthians 12:7-10** and write in your own words what God's provision was to Paul in relation to this "weakness" he was experiencing.

____

____

____

God's response to Paul was that He would continue to give Paul grace (the unmerited favor and love of God), and His grace was sufficient enough to meet Paul's every need. How has the Lord's grace and subsequent strength been revealed to you through your weaknesses?

____

____

____

In order to experience God's strength on a daily basis, we must set our minds on Jesus, recognize that He alone sustains us, and allow the sanctifying power of the Holy Spirit to work within us. What are some practical steps you can take in order to experience this power and boast as Paul did, "when I am weak, then I am strong"?

____

____

____

Trusting God and knowing that He is consistently weaving His perfect plan into place despite our weaknesses is sometimes unfathomable to imagine. Read Psalm 46:10. In the midst of your stillness and recognizing the HOPE He alone brings, what is the Holy Spirit speaking to you?

____

____

____

For your small group time:

Opening Up and Being Real

Build community within your small group as you discuss the themes of the podcast.

- What resonated with you about Courtney's story? Why?

- Courtney spoke about going to her first Bible study group and how it "gave her a taste of something she had not previously known," and she was "sold out." Have you ever studied God's Word and felt the Holy Spirit move in a way that left you hungry for more? If so, can you share your experience with the group?

- Courtney also said as she listened to the women in the Bible study tell their stories she thought, "I don't have a story like that." But then, she followed her comment with the fact she didn't know God as Redeemer. How can knowing your Father in Heaven as Redeemer help you to see more of Him in your own story? What does the term "Redeemer" mean to you?

- Early on in her Christian walk, Courtney spoke about knowing God as a God who would reward or punish her based on her behavior, so she tried to be a "good girl" in her formative years. Later on in her life, when her world began to crumble, she reverted back to her old ways of viewing God, thinking maybe she was being punished for all the wrong choices she had made. Have you ever viewed the struggles in your life as judgment from God for past sin? How can knowing God as a merciful, sovereign Father change your way of thinking?

- It's easy, as Courtney did, to pull away from God in the midst of terrible suffering or tragedy. Has there been a time in your life (or maybe you are in the midst of one now) where you have pulled away from God because you didn't understand His ways? How can Isaiah 55:8-9 give us comfort in those moments?

- At one point in her story, Courtney said, "I thought everyone's life was fine and mine was not, and I was embarrassed and ashamed." Have you ever felt this way about your life? How does our world of social media feed into this lie?

- As Courtney shared about meeting Tim in the auto repair shop, she saw how God used that meeting to bring hope to her son who was in prison and then that led to favor on her son. Have you ever seen the Lord's favor in a situation you were praying over? Share with the group if you can.

- A large part of Courtney's story was about the many masks she hid behind to camouflage what was really going on in her life. What masks have you put on (or are you putting on) to try to hide behind? What made you (or makes you) reach for those masks? Why do you think it becomes easy to spot the masks other people are wearing when ours are removed?

- Trusting God and recognizing His plan is perfect was how Courtney was finally able to surrender to God and take off her many masks. Are you completely trusting God today? If so, how did you get to this point in your spiritual walk? If not, what is holding you back?

Closing Your Small Group Time with Prayer

Spend time in worship as you reflect on what God has taught you through the storyteller and His Word.

Take time as a group to pray in any of the following directions:

Praise God for the story He brought you through Courtney. Praise Him for His goodness and His acceptance. Praise Him for sending His Son Jesus and for being your Redeemer.

Ask God for forgiveness when you have hidden behind masks and trusted in your own abilities instead of putting on the armor of God. Ask God to forgive you when you have doubted His sovereignty and His plan for your life. Ask Him to forgive you when you have acted as if you don't trust Him and His ways.

Thank God for allowing your story to be part of His bigger story and for the opportunity to serve Him through your story. Thank Him for being a Father who continually reaches out to you and draws you closer to Him. Thank Him for His Word that says if we draw close to Him, He will draw near to us (James 4:8).

Pray God would help you to see the masks you are hiding behind. Pray God would allow you to completely understand that your strength comes from Him and you are an overcomer because of it. Pray God would increase your trust in Him and His plan for your life and the ones you love.

SESSION SIX

AMY G

"Healing Through the Heartache of Losing a Child"

> *"'For I know the plans I have for you.' declares the Lord, 'plans to prosper you and not harm you, plans to give you hope and a future'"*
> Jeremiah 29:11

When God shows up, you discover He can bring healing to your soul.

Think About It

Questions to consider before and after you listen to the podcast.

Have you ever questioned God's goodness? If so, what brought about your questioning?

____

____

____

How can questioning God actually draw you closer to Him?

____

____

____

Listen to the Podcast

"Amy G: Healing Through the Heartache of Losing a Child"
Find the podcast at www.storytellerslive.org/storiesofhope

StoryTeller Podcast Highlights

- Every time I share my story, a part of my heart is healed.
- This wasn't our plan, but it was God's.
- You have every right to be mad, but it's how you handle the anger from here on out.
- "I am bigger than your anger. Be mad at Me. I can handle it, and I still love you." And, in an instant, the anger was gone.
- "You are still worth celebrating and that's why I'm saying happy birthday."
- We share our story in hopes that others will make it to Jesus.

Study the Story in Scripture

Allow God's Word to transform your heart, mind, and soul as you spend time alone with Him.

The death of a loved one, especially the death of a child, is devastating and can lead one into despair. The beautiful gift God gives you in these moments is that He wants to walk alongside you. He doesn't expect you to catch up to Him, and He doesn't get frustrated when you feel angry or sad. He meets you right where you are to give you strength for each step. How can these verses bring you hope in grief?

Luke 1:78-79

____

____

Romans 6:5

____

____

Psalm 107:13-14

____

____

Revelation 14:13

____

____

How can 2 Corinthians 4:8-18 bring you comfort when grieving a loved one's passing?

____

____

Read Jeremiah 29:11 with fresh eyes. How does this verse speak specifically to you today?

____

____

____

Focusing on the promises of God was how Amy found comfort in her grief. Read Isaiah 41:10. What two things does this verse tell you to NOT DO? What two things does it tell you God WILL DO? How can you hold onto these four statements in times of suffering?

____

____

____

Amy experienced healing through incredible heartache. Write out what the following verses say about God and healing.

Mark 5:34

____

____

Deuteronomy 32:39

____

____

Job 5:18

____

____

Psalm 147:3

____

____

____

Acts 28:27

____

____

____

Do you have other verses you cling to in moments of sorrow? If so, write them out and reflect on the grace and mercy God gives you through His Word.

____

____

____

____

____

Choosing joy in difficult circumstances is not easy. Read 1 Thessalonians 5:16-18. What are the three things God's Word tells you to do? How can you practice these three commands even in the midst of trials?

____

____

____

____

____

As Christians, we know in this world we will suffer, but we suffer with hope. Hope in knowing an eternal home awaits us. Amy ended with three verses that remind her of God's love and our eternal home. Revisit the following verses and write a prayer of thankfulness to God of what awaits you as a believer: Romans 8:18, 1 Corinthians 2:9, Revelation 21:4

Dear God... ____

____

____

For your small group time:

Opening Up and Being Real

Build community within your small group as you discuss the themes of the podcast.

- What resonated with you about Amy's story? Why?

- Amy opened by saying, "Every time I share my story, a part of me is healed." God created us to share our struggles and long-sufferings with one another. Can you tell about a time when you experienced healing after sharing your pain with others?

- Amy spoke several times about how others helped her and her husband carry their burden after Ann Reese's passing. God created us for community. How have you experienced this community in your life?

- After the loss of a loved one, anger is a natural emotion to experience. Amy's pastor said, "It's what you do with that anger that matters." What do you think he meant by that?

- Amy heard God say to her, "Be mad at me. I can handle it, and I still love you." What does this statement stir up in you? How is questioning God more productive than being mad at Him?

- Writing (journaling) was a pathway of healing for Amy. Do you write/ journal to God? If so, have you experienced healing in your life through this avenue?

- The number 18 was a "God-wink" to Amy and her family. Do you have any "God winks" you can share?

- Amy said God has taught her and her husband how to choose joy through the hurt and the pain. How can you choose joy each day?

Closing Your Small Group Time with Prayer

Spend time in worship as you reflect on what God has taught you through the storyteller and His Word.

Take time as a group to pray in any of the following directions:

Praise God for the story He brought you through Amy. Praise Him for being a God who can heal you through devastating loss and heartache. Praise Him for being a Heavenly Father who allows you to be mad at Him and can handle your anger and loves you through it all.

Ask God for forgiveness when you have lived out of your anger towards Him instead of expressing your anger to Him.

Thank God for the life of Ann Reese. Thank Him for the "God-winks" He showed Amy and for the "God-winks" in your life. Thank God for the gift of community. Thank Him for the specific people in your life who have helped you carry the burdens of your life.

Pray God would help you to view life from an eternal perspective. Ask Him to heal the areas of you life where you have experienced heartache. Pray God would supernaturally equip you to choose joy in the midst of grief and pain.

SESSION SEVEN

RACHEL

"Experiencing God Through a Spouse's Addiction"

> *"Come to me, all you who are weary and burdened,*
> *and I will give you rest."*
> Matthew 11:28

When God shows up, you discover you can forgive others and celebrate redemption.

Think About It

Questions to consider before and after you listen to the podcast.

Have you ever faced a battle in your life where you had to rely completely on God?

____

____

____

How do you react when someone you love deeply disappoints you?

____

____

____

Listen to the Podcast

"Rachel: Experiencing God Through a Spouse's Addiction"
Find the podcast at www.storytellerslive.org/storiesofhope

StoryTeller Podcast Highlights

- We had no idea what we were up against.
- Focus on His truth. He's going to meet all my needs, not some, but all.
- The fear that gripped me ... we would pretend everything was good.
- I know You are in this, and I know You will carry us through.
- I was burdened and exhausted, but I would hear God say, I'm going to use you. I'm going to use you."
- No matter what you face, it doesn't have to be addiction, God is faithful and what His Word says is true.

Study the Story in Scripture

Allow God's Word to transform your heart, mind, and soul as you spend time alone with Him.

Our lives are filled with various forms of temptations, but as long as we look to God, His Word promises us that He will provide a way of escape in tempting times. It's important to note that He will never force us to use the way of escape, but, rest assured, He will make sure it is available. God leaves the choice to us as to whether we take His way of escape or not. How can the following verses bring you strength when you are trying to overcome the desires of your flesh?

1 Corinthians 10:13-14

James 4:7

Titus 2:11-14

Hebrews 4:15-16

2 Peter 1 is a great reminder of the divine power you have as a believer in Jesus Christ. This chapter lists seven qualities to add to your faith so you will be effective and productive in your knowledge of Jesus Christ. What are those seven qualities?

____

____

____

Review 2 Peter 1:10-11. How can confirming your calling and visualizing your rich welcome into God's "eternal kingdom" help you live out of your spirit and not your flesh?

____

____

____

Read Romans 12:1-2. What does the Apostle Paul ask you to do? What will you see at the end of this transformation?

____

____

____

When we are weary and burdened, we tend to continue relying on ourselves to get through our struggles. Read Matthew 11:28-30 and write out what Jesus offers.

____

____

____

How can you take steps to pick up Jesus' yoke and learn from Him so you can experience rest in times of deep despair?

____

____

____

How has God used others in times of hardship to bring you rest?

____

____

____

In the beginning of Rachel's story, she said God was so faithful and sweet to bring back the memories of the hard times so she could see how God has moved in her family. Take a moment and reflect on the hard times in your life and how God has moved. Write a prayer of thanksgiving for His faithfulness.

____

____

____

While your past is history, it is also HIS story. Rachel could clearly see this once she and Brian were on the other side. How can seeing your story as God's bring you hope in your everyday life?

____

____

____

For your small group time:

Opening Up and Being Real

Build community within your small group as you discuss the themes of the podcast.

- What resonated with you about Rachel's story? Why?

- When Rachel first learned of her husband's addiction, her initial reaction was, "Well...you just need to fix that." Have you ever had that feeling towards yourself or someone you loved? Did it work?

- Rachel said she would hope and pray no one would find out about Brian's addiction. Why do you think we tend to hide our struggles instead of sharing them and asking for help?

- When Brian went to his first treatment facility, Rachel said she was sad, but by the second time, she was furious. Have you ever experienced this type of disappointment with a loved one's failed attempts to change? How did you handle your disappointment?

- During Brian's second treatment, Rachel experienced fear that would grip her, but, she would tell God, "I know you are in this and will carry us through." How has God carried you in times of fear or deep disappointment?

- How does Rachel's statement "I knew God, but I hadn't experienced God" speak to you?

- Rachel said as she reflects on where her family has been, she takes nothing for granted (her electricity being on, money to buy pizzas, etc.). How can thankfulness keep our eyes focused on Jesus?

Closing Your Small Group Time with Prayer

Spend time in worship as you reflect on what God has taught you through the storyteller and His Word.

Take time as a group to pray in any of the following directions:

Praise God for the story He brought you through Rachel. Praise Him for the work He is doing and continues to do through Brian's story of deliverance. Praise God for being a God of countless chances - an ever-forgiving, all-loving Father. Praise Him for being a Father who meets all (not just some, but all) of your needs.

Ask God for forgiveness when you have allowed the desires of your flesh to direct your life. Ask Him for forgiveness for the times when you haven't gone directly to Him for guidance and help in your life. Ask Him for forgiveness when you have lived out of fear.

Thank God for being a Father you can go to when you are weary and burdened and for the promise of rest in those moments. Thank Him for His faithfulness in the midst of the trials you face, and for the courage He provides when you are gripped with fear. Thank Him for the gift of deliverance and transformation and for molding you into a new creation.

Pray God would help you to overcome the desires of your flesh. If you are in a stage of life where fear has gripped you, ask God to be your strength and your comfort, and ask Him to increase your trust in Him. Ask God to help you offer your body as a living sacrifice, holy and pleasing to Him. Pray He would continue to transform you by the renewing of your mind. Ask Him to allow you to not only know Him, but to experience Him.

SESSION EIGHT

KRISTIN

"Freedom from Fear"

"For the Spirit God gave us does not make us timid, but gives us power, love and self-discipline."
2 Timothy 1:7

When God shows up, you discover all fears are gone!

Think About It

Questions to consider before and after you listen to the podcast.

How can shame paralyze you in your relationship with God and with others?

____

____

____

Why do we allow fear to dictate our actions?

____

____

____

Listen to the Podcast

"Kristin: Freedom From Fear"
Find the podcast at www.storytellerslive.org/storiesofhope

StoryTeller Podcast Highlights

- Built up a lot of walls. The safety zone I had created for her and for me was just gone in an instant. I was just lost.
- I was living the dream, but I wasn't happy, and I didn't like myself. I had so much shame and fear.
- I thought, I'm ending it all or I need help." I chose help.
- Big part of healing was allowing myself to be open. God lays things on my heart and tells me to share it.
- I now know the things that scare me the most, when I do them, that's when I see God.
- "Fear is a self-imposed prison that will keep you from becoming what God intends for you to be. You must move against it with weapons of faith and hope." - Rick Warren

Study the Story in Scripture

In her story, Kristin explained that for a large part of her life she had a false view of God. An incorrect view of God and His ways can be a common occurrence among many of God's children. Some false views can be thinking God is a God who is impossible to please; or God is a condemning dictator; or He is a God who can't possibly forgive our shortcomings; or God is distant and unavailable. In order for us to grow in our relationship with God, we must correct our incorrect ways of thinking. What do the following verses tell us about our Heavenly Father?

1 Corinthians 1:9

____

____

2 Corinthians 1:3-4

____

____

Matthew 7:9-11

____

____

1 John 4:9-10; 16

____

____

Psalm 3:3

____

____

Psalm 103:10-14

____

____

Philippians 4:19

____

____

Proverbs 18:10

____

____

Satan is known as the father of lies, (John 8:44) and fear is a lie he consistently uses. As believers, by the name of Jesus Christ who lives in us, we've been given authority over fear. Many verses in the book of Psalms speak of fear and how to combat it. Read the following verses and write out what they say about God's protection over Satan's greatest lie.

Psalm 23:4

____

____

Psalm 27:1-3

____

____

Psalm 34:4

____

____

Psalm 46:1

____

____

Psalm 56:3

____

____

Psalm 91:1-16

____

____

Now that you've looked up who God is and what His Word says about fear, how can you place your security and trust in Him when He calls you to do something you feel ill-equipped to do?

____

____

____

We must fight Satan's lies with spiritual weapons. Read Ephesians 6 and write down the weapons God gives us to fight with during spiritual warfare.

____

____

____

Read 2 Timothy 1:7-8. How do these verses speak to you?

____

____

____

In the previous Scripture, Paul tells Timothy to not be ashamed of the testimony about our Lord. As a result, we should be telling everyone we know what the Lord has done for us. Read 1 Peter 3:15. How does this verse encourage you to tell your story (testimony of Christ and His love) to others? What, if anything, is holding you back?

____

____

____

Each of the stories over the past eight weeks has focused on the hope God desires for us to live from. A famous hymn, tided, "_The Solid Rock_" speaks of where to find this hope and how to build your life around it. The first stanza and chorus say: "_My hope is built on nothing less than Jesus' blood and righteousness. I dare not trust the sweetest frame but wholly lean on Jesus' name. On Christ, the solid rock, I stand; all other ground is sinking sand, all other ground is sinking sand._" After going through this study, how do these words speak to you today?

____

____

____

For your small group time:

Opening Up and Being Real

Build community within your small group as you discuss the themes of the podcast.

- What resonated with you about Kristin's story? Why?

- What walls have you put up in relationships in order to protect yourself?

- Early on, Kristin placed her trust in the "safety zone" she had created between her and her mom. Have you ever put your trust in a person or thing creating a false sense of security? What was the result?

- Like Kristin, have you ever found yourself "living the dream" but you weren't happy? If so, in those moments, what were your thoughts and subsequent actions?
- Kristin was living in guilt as she was waiting for her life to come crashing down so she could blame herself. How are we our own worse enemy at times?

- A neighbor stepped out in faith and asked Kristin to join her small group. What holds you back from asking others to join you at your small group or your church?

- As Christians, all of us have full access to the power of God through His Holy Spirit, but we must choose to use it. What holds you back from tapping into this power?

- What's the scariest thing God has called you to do, and if you followed through, what did He teach you?

- What is God calling you to do today and fear is holding you back?

Closing Your Small Group Time with Prayer

Spend time in worship as you reflect on what God has taught you through the storyteller and His Word.

Take time as a group to pray in any of the following directions:

Praise God for the story He brought you through Kristin. Praise Him for His Holy Spirit that gives you power, love, and self-discipline. Praise God for the privilege of approaching His throne in prayer. Praise Him for being the "name above all names," especially the name of "fear."

Ask God for forgiveness for any false views you have had (or have) of Him (pray He would reveal those false views). Ask Him to forgive you when you have placed yourself in a "self-imposed" prison and lived out of fear, guilt, or shame. Ask God for forgiveness for the times in your life where you didn't trust Him or believe Him.

Thank God for giving the unimaginable gift of Jesus so you can have access to the power of the Holy Spirit. Thank Him for the fruit of His Spirit: love, joy, peace, patience, kindness, goodness, faithfulness, gentleness, and self-control. Thank Him for hearing your prayers and honoring them, and thank Him for working in advance.

Pray God would help you to break down any walls in your life you have created. Pray He would help you to relinquish any shame or fear you have in your life. Pray God would equip you to take the steps of faith toward Him, and that you would experience Him as you take those steps. Pray for the courage to follow through with what God is calling you to do.

FIND YOUR COMMUNITY

One of the prayers we have for the women who go through "When God Shows Up" is for this Bible study to catapult you to realizing you need a group of believers to do life with... a safe place where walls can be torn down and vulnerability can rise up.

We believe the church body is the perfect place to start! We encourage you to find a group of believers and get involved in a local church.

Or, are you already a member of a church and it's been a while since you got involved? Let this study be a jumping point for you to get back into church and use the gifts God has given you to serve.

Need 3 easy ways to bring this study to your church?

Offer the StoryTellers Live Bible studies to your women's ministry

Present a "Discover Your Story" Workshop by StoryTellers Live

Host a "Your Story Matters" conference

How to support StoryTellers Live:

Check out all of the StoryTellers Live Biblical resources at storytellerslive.org/shop

Consider a donation at storytellerslive.org/give

Join our Patreon community for extra content at patreon.com/STLcommunity

If you are interested in starting an STL community
or if you just want more information about Storytellers, email us at

info@storytellerslive.org

IRON HILL

press

Equipping the Church
to know God
through His Word.

ironhillpress.com | 800.307.9366